pasta sauces

pasta sauces

Lindy Wildsmith

photography by Nicky Dowey

RYLAND
PETERS
& SMALL
LONDON NEW YORK

Published in the United States in 2004
by Ryland Peters & Small, Inc.
519 Broadway, 5th Floor, New York, NY 1001
www.rylandpeters.com

10 9 8 7 6 5 4 3 2 1

Library of Congress Cataloging-in-Publication Data

Wildsmith, Lindy.
  Pasta sauces / Lindy Wildsmith ; photography by Nicky Dowey.
    p. cm.
  ISBN 1-84172-576-5
1. Sauces. 2. Cookery (Pasta) I. Title.
  TX819.A1.W54 2004
  641.8'14--dc21

                            2003013205

Printed and bound in China

Notes
•All spoon measurements are level unless otherwise specified.
•Fresh herbs are used in this book unless otherwise stated. If using
dried herbs, halve the quantity given.
•All eggs are large, unless otherwise specified. Uncooked or partially
cooked eggs should not be served to the very young, the very old,
those with compromised immune systems, or to pregnant women.

Designers Susan Downing, Luana Gobbo

Commissioning Editor Elsa Petersen-Schepelern

Editor Susan Stuck

Production Deborah Wehner

Art Director Gabriella Le Grazie

Publishing Director Alison Starling

Food Stylist Lucy McKelvie

Stylist Antonia Gaunt

contents

pasta and sauces for pasta

This is my collection of favorite pasta sauces. Many are classics, gleaned from friends in Italy over the years and known to lovers of Italian food everywhere. Others are my own invention, inspired by seasonal produce and the authentic Italian ingredients now available the world over. All are strongly rooted in the traditions of delicious Italian regional cooking.

Some sauces take no time at all to prepare, involve very little cooking, and are more like dressings than sauces. In fact, the word *condimento* (dressing) comes to mind; the Italians often use it rather than *salsa* or *sugo* (sauce) when talking about pasta. Other sauces, particularly meat sauces, can be prepared in advance (a plus when having friends over), then reheated when required. Many have pantry equivalents, which are great for unexpected guests and "home-from-work, straight-onto-the-table" meals. All are easy to make—the choice is yours.

A mound of freshly cooked pasta oozing with your favorite sauce, glistening with Parmesan cheese, makes the perfect meal for family and friends. Add a salad, some fruit and cheese, maybe a *gelato affogato* (ice cream drowning in liqueur), and coffee—serve it all at a pretty table and you have an instant party.

Which sauce for which pasta?

Homemade pasta made with eggs and wheat flour comes from the north of Italy. The sauces that are served with it are, on the whole, rich meat- and dairy-based sauces enhanced with Parmesan cheese, reflecting the rich agricultural heritage of the north. Spaghetti made with durum wheat flour, cultivated in the more arid south, comes originally from Naples. Myriad homemade pasta shapes, made with this flour, water, and the

spirit of invention brought by necessity, are set in the traditions of the cooking of the south. Here, in the land of sunshine, tomatoes and vegetables thrived. Olives, in the form of oil, provided the fat of the land.

Tradition is still at the heart of authentic Italian food and there is a simple rule to follow when deciding which pasta to serve with which sauce. Egg pasta, long or short, is perfect for sauces based on dairy food and meat, while spaghetti and other pasta shapes made with durum wheat are more suited to the lighter olive-oil-based sauces made with fish and vegetables.

Cream and meat sauces also go well with ridged tubes, especially if there are small delicious bits to be trapped inside. Ridged pasta is particularly good for creamy sauces, as there is more surface area for the sauce to bind itself to.

One last word—don't be afraid to try different sauces with different pastas and find out what you like!

Buying pasta

When buying dried pasta, stick to Italian brands. Supermarkets have them, and you can also be sure that any store serving an Italian community will have a good range of top-quality, Italian-made pasta at a reasonable price and lots of shapes to choose from. Designer pasta in funky shapes and colors makes a fun gift, but stick to basics when buying for yourself.

No need, either, to buy fresh pasta (other than the stuffed variety). Good-quality, Italian-made dried egg pasta is better than most bought fresh pasta and it is what Italians use most of the time. I always check the labeling to make sure it's made in Italy—some manufacturers in other countries do not have the same exacting standards. If you make your own pasta, it's fantastic, but be warned—it's two hours in the making, two minutes in the eating.

Cooking pasta

To cook pasta successfully, you need plenty of salted boiling water; 5 quarts of water and 3 tablespoons of coarse sea salt for every 16 oz. of pasta. Bring the salted water to a rolling boil, add the pasta, bring back to a boil, stir again, and stir from time to time. Follow the cooking times on the package, but start tasting at least 2 minutes before the cooking time is up. It should still have bite to it—known in Italian as *al dente* or "to the tooth."

As soon as the pasta is ready, strain it through a colander, reserving a cupful of the pasta water. This is useful for diluting pestos and cheese dressings. I always return at least 2 tablespoons of this cooking water back to the pasta when adding the sauce, because it helps stir it in.

For sauces based on meat or vegetables, strain the pasta back into the saucepan, add the sauce, and mix well. For sauces based on cream, cheese, or eggs, strain the pasta into a large bowl and add the sauce. (This kind of sauce dries out too much in the heat of the pan.)

Dress all pasta as you would a salad and spend plenty of time over it. Add lots of extra Parmesan, herbs, olive oil, and other flavorings before serving, and a dish of extra Parmesan on the table is always welcome.

How much?

Most of my recipes suggest that a 16 oz. package of pasta is sufficient for 4-6 people as an entrée, and 6-8 people for an appetizer. How much pasta and how much sauce to use is very much a question of taste. In Italy, 4 oz. is generally considered a typical portion for one person and is served coated in sauce, but not swimming in it, and not hidden under it—and this is how I like to serve pasta. I nearly always cook a 16 oz. package of pasta and dress it all.

If there is any left over, it can be reheated the next day in the microwave (covered closely with plastic wrap). If you prefer it with more sauce and less pasta, simply adapt the quantities to taste.

Olive oil

I use a good extra virgin olive oil for all cooking other than sautéing, but I also keep a small bottle of something a little bit special for dishes where the flavor of the oil is tantamount. My favorites are the oils from Liguria, Le Marche, Puglia, and Sicily, or from a named olive variety such as Taggiasca.

Olive oil should be used within 18 months of production, because it will become rancid, especially when exposed to light and heat. Either buy it in a can or store the bottle in a cool, dark place and decant it into a stainless steel or ceramic pourer for regular kitchen and table use.

Most people come back from Italy with handbags, shoes, and designer labels. I usually turn up at the airport with olive oil, salami, and a new cooking pot or skillet, much to the hilarity of the security staff.

Tomatoes

When choosing tomatoes, make sure they are firm to the touch and have a light bloom on the skin—and don't forget to smell them! Discover where they were grown and, whenever possible, buy tomatoes ripened in the sun and not forced out of season.

Although we associate beef and plum tomatoes with Italy, they are not necessarily a good choice in other parts of the world, where they can often be pithy and flavorless. Put them and vine tomatoes through this same test—all are more expensive, but don't necessarily taste better.

Having said this, I use Italian *pellati* (canned peeled tomatoes, whole or in "fillets") for all my cooked tomato sauces. You can be sure they are sun-ripened and flavorful.

Wheat and other intolerances

Can't eat wheat? Don't worry. Wheat-free, gluten-free pasta made from cornmeal is definitely worth a try. Problems with dairy? Try adding chopped herbs or nuts instead of Parmesan cheese or, even better, bread crumbs, sautéed with garlic and herbs.

For vegetarians, the choice is huge, and where I have added chopped meats to recipes based on vegetables or cheese, use ingredients such as sun-dried tomatoes, capers, olives, and nuts instead. Fish eaters can add smoked fish and anchovies.

Buon appetito!

classics

Classic pasta sauces have their origins in the traditional cooking of regional Italy. Some of them are uniquely linked to one region, while some feature in the cooking of many regions and there are many versions of the same recipe. Share your favorite with an Italian and he will tell you, you've got it wrong; his will be better, however authentic yours may be. So, when talking food—and in Italy you can't avoid it—be ready to listen.

tomato sauce with vegetables
condimento di pomodoro e verdure

This useful base sauce is the first tomato sauce I learned to make when I lived in Bologna, in the north of Italy. It begins with a classic *battuto* (chopping) of carrot, onion, and celery, used often in Italian cooking. This sauce is more substantial and has a stronger flavor than the Neapolitan recipe on page 13. It is also the best recipe for non-plum tomatoes, because the vegetable base gives the extra flavor that other tomato varieties lack.

To prepare the tomatoes, cut a cross in the base of each one, squeeze out the seeds, and discard them.

Heat the butter and olive oil in a heavy saucepan over high heat. When it starts to bubble, add the celery, carrot, onion, herbs, and tomatoes. Stir quickly in the hot fat for a few minutes, then lower the heat, cover, and simmer for 1 hour. Stir from time to time, adding a little water as the tomatoes reduce.

Push the sauce though a food mill or sieve. Add salt and pepper to taste.

Toss the sauce through the pasta, then add Parmesan, sprinkle with torn or chopped herbs and olive oil. Serve extra Parmesan separately for people to help themselves.

Notes

• When plum tomatoes are out of season, Italian cooks use *pellati* (canned peeled tomatoes). Make sure you use a good brand, preferably Italian—buy whole, rather than chopped, to ensure quality.

• This sauce can be made in bulk and frozen in batches.

16 oz. pasta, such as fusilli, or stuffed pasta, freshly cooked

tomato and vegetable sauce

2 lb. fresh plum tomatoes, about 6 medium

2 tablespoons unsalted butter

2 tablespoons olive oil

1 small celery stalk, finely chopped

1 small carrot, finely chopped

1 small onion, finely chopped

a small bunch of basil or other herbs, chopped

sea salt and freshly ground black pepper

to serve

a handful of fresh herbs, torn or finely chopped

extra virgin olive oil

freshly grated Parmesan cheese

serves 4–6

11

quick neapolitan tomato sauce
il sugo di pomodoro

This classic tomato sauce comes originally from Campania, the region around Naples. The great nineteenth-century Italian food writer, Pellegrino Artusi, believed it to be beneficial to the digestive system; it certainly goes down a treat. It is made simply with tomatoes, olive oil, garlic, and the flavoring of your choice. I use Italian canned plum tomatoes, making it a handy pantry standby.

Put the prepared tomatoes, oil, and garlic in a heavy saucepan. Add your choice of the chile, cinnamon, and dried or fresh herbs. Cover and simmer over low heat for 30 minutes, or until the tomatoes are reduced to a creamy mass.

Stir from time to time to keep the sauce from sticking to the bottom of the pan. Add a little of the reserved tomato juice whenever necessary to keep the sauce moist. Discard the garlic and chile, cinnamon, or herbs. Mash the sauce with a potato masher. If using fresh herbs, it may be necessary to purée the sauce in a blender. Taste and adjust the seasoning with salt and freshly ground black pepper.

Pour the sauce over the freshly cooked pasta, top with the Parmesan, and stir well. Transfer to a serving dish, sprinkle with fresh herbs, if using, then serve at once with extra cheese and olive oil.

Variations

• Chop 8 oz. fresh mozzarella cheese into small cubes and stir through the pasta at the same time as the Parmesan. Add a handful of torn basil leaves to the bowl and stir well before serving.

• Serve trenette pasta with this tomato sauce alongside trenette with Pesto Genovese (page 18).

16 oz. pasta, dried, fresh, or stuffed, freshly cooked

tomato sauce

2 cans plum tomatoes, about 14 oz. each, seeded, drained (reserve the juice), and chopped

⅓ cup extra virgin olive oil

4 garlic cloves

your choice of:
1 small piece of fresh chile,
½ cinnamon stick,
½ teaspoon dried oregano,
or a bunch of fresh herbs such as basil

3 tablespoons freshly grated Parmesan cheese

sea salt and freshly ground black pepper

to serve

a handful of fresh herbs, torn or finely chopped (optional)

freshly grated Parmesan cheese

extra virgin olive oil

serves 4–6

aglio, olio e peperoncino
garlic, olive oil and chile

If you like spicy and simple food, this is for you. It is a typical dish of the mountainous Abruzzo region, where long snowy winters have inspired all kinds of warming specialities popular with the skiers who flock there. Local fiery chiles, or *diavolini* (little devils) as they are called, are added to many of the region's dishes, salami, and cured meats. Make this dressing swiftly, cook the pasta *al dente*, use the best-quality ingredients, and serve straight away. Serve as an appetizer until you become a connoisseur.

12 oz. pasta, such as spaghettini or penne, freshly cooked

freshly grated Parmesan cheese (optional), to serve

garlic dressing

⅔ cup very best olive oil

4 garlic cloves, peeled but whole

1 teaspoon dried hot red pepper flakes

2 handfuls of parsley, finely chopped

serves 4–6 as an appetizer

While the pasta is boiling, slowly heat the olive oil in a skillet with the garlic and pepper flakes. When the garlic turns golden, discard it. Drain the pasta, then return it to the saucepan. Add the hot flavored oil, pepper flakes, and chopped parsley and stir well. Serve at once, with Parmesan, if using.

Variations

Arrabbiata

For spice lovers, this is a tomato-based version of the first recipe. The word *arrabbiata* means "rabid" and is used in Italian to mean "angry." It is a popular dish in Rome and generally made on demand in simple eateries. Use the tomato sauce recipe on page 13 (Quick Neapolitan Tomato Sauce), but double the amount of garlic and chiles. Add 2 handfuls of parsley, finely chopped, at the end.

Amatriciana

This sauce is very similar to Arrabbiata, but contains an onion instead of garlic and has a pancetta base. It is featured in the meat and poultry section on page 47.

ragù
rich meat sauce from Bologna

People tell me they have had spaghetti with meat sauce on holiday in Italy—and so they might, but never (no never) in Bologna. Spaghetti bolognese is the original fusion dish, an invention as British as roast beef. In Bologna they serve *ragù,* as it is called (not Bolognese sauce), with tagliatelle or rigatoni, but never with spaghetti—and it does make a difference. They do have a *salsa bolognese* (Bolognese sauce), but it is made with oranges and Marsala wine and served with duck.

Heat the oil and butter in a heavy saucepan over medium heat. Add the chopped carrot, celery, onion, and pancetta and cook until transparent. Increase the heat, add the meat, and sauté until browned. Add the wine and let bubble until evaporated.

Lower the heat, add enough milk to cover the meat, then add the tomato paste and nutmeg. Cook rapidly until the milk has reduced by at least half. Lower the heat, top up with enough warm stock or water to cover the meat, stir, cover with a lid, and simmer for at least 1 hour. Stir from time to time.

Add salt and pepper to taste, then set aside to rest overnight to develop the flavors.

When ready to serve, reheat the sauce and add to the freshly cooked pasta. Stir in the cheese, parsley, and the 2 tablespoons butter and serve with extra cheese.

Variation

Make double the quantity of sauce and freeze half.

16 oz. long or short egg pasta, or rigatoni, freshly cooked

ragù sauce

1 tablespoon olive oil

2 tablespoons unsalted butter

1 small carrot, finely chopped

1 small celery stalk, finely chopped

1 small onion, finely chopped.

4 slices pancetta, prosciutto, or bacon, ground, about ½ cup

1 lb. ground beef, sirloin or round

2 tablespoons white wine

1½ cups whole milk, or enough to cover the meat

1½ tablespoons tomato paste

½ nutmeg, freshly grated

1–2 cups warm stock or water

sea salt and freshly ground black pepper

to serve

½ cup freshly grated Parmesan cheese, plus extra to taste

3 tablespoons freshly chopped flat-leaf parsley

2 tablespoons unsalted butter

serves 4–6

pesto genovese

16 oz. egg pasta, such as trenette or penne, freshly cooked

pesto

a handful of pine nuts

1 walnut half

1 small garlic clove

a pinch of salt

1 teaspoon unsalted butter

a large, leafy bunch of basil

²∕₃–1 cup olive oil

1½ tablespoons freshly grated pecorino cheese

1½ tablespoons freshly grated Parmesan cheese

to serve

extra virgin olive oil

freshly grated Parmesan cheese

serves 4–6

*In Italy, it's traditional to count the basil leaves—there should be 70 small leaves or 35 large.

Pesto is from Liguria in northern Italy—basil, olive oil, Parmesan and pecorino cheeses, pine nuts, and garlic are ground together to form an aromatic pasta dressing. Traditionally, pesto was made with a mortar and pestle. Purists say never put a metal blade to a basil leaf—tear rather than chop the leaves to prevent them from discoloring. Adding a little butter to your pesto will help preserve its vivid green color. It is tempting to buy it rather than make your own, but freshly made pesto is very special and, with the help of a blender, simple to do. Make it in the spring and summer when basil is in season and sold in big leafy bunches, heavy with peppery scent.

To make the pesto, put the pine nuts in a dry skillet and heat gently until golden brown all over. Take care, because they burn easily. Remove to a plate and let cool.

When cool, put the pine nuts, walnut, garlic, salt, and butter in a blender and blend well. Add the basil and blend until smooth. Add the oil and reduce to a paste, then add the two cheeses quickly at the end.

Transfer the pesto to a serving dish, then rinse out the blender with a couple of tablespoons of pasta water and add to the pesto. Transfer the freshly cooked pasta to the dish of pesto, pour over the olive oil, sprinkle with cheese, and mix well.

Variations

• Make a double quantity of pesto, store in a screw-top jar, seal with a layer of olive oil, and refrigerate.

• Mix in freshly cooked spring vegetables such as asparagus spears cut into short lengths, fava beans, peas, or green beans. Alternatively, stir in a tomato salad, such as the one on page 43.

puttanesca

streetwalker's sauce

This is from Campania, from the island of Ischia, but why it's called streetwalker's sauce, I don't know. Suffice to say, the combination of the local ingredients—olive oil, garlic, chiles, anchovies, tomatoes, olives, and capers—packs a real punch and would warm the cockles of your heart, whatever your profession.

Cover the base of a medium saucepan with olive oil (traditionally the pan would have been made of terracotta). Add the garlic and pepper flakes and set over low heat. Remove the garlic clove as soon as it starts to turn golden. Add the mashed anchovies, chopped tomatoes, capers, olives, and black pepper. Stir and continue cooking until the sauce has reduced and darkened in color, about 20-30 minutes. If the sauce starts to dry out too much, stir in a little of the reserved tomato juice.

Add the sauce to the freshly cooked pasta and stir well. Transfer to a large serving dish, add the parsley and oil, and serve at once.

16 oz. pasta, such as spaghetti, penne or cavatappi, freshly cooked

puttanesca sauce

olive oil, for cooking

1 large garlic clove, finely chopped

1 teaspoon hot red pepper flakes

1 small can anchovy fillets, about 2 oz., drained and mashed

2 cans peeled plum tomatoes, 14 oz. each, drained (reserve the juice), seeded, and chopped

2 oz. capers (if salted rinse well and pat dry with paper towels)

½ cup good imported black olives, such as cerignola

freshly ground black pepper

to serve

2 handfuls of parsley, finely chopped

extra virgin olive oil

serves 4–6

carbonara

16 oz. pasta, such as spaghetti or penne, freshly cooked

carbonara sauce

2 whole eggs

5 egg yolks

2 tablespoons unsalted butter

½ cup light cream

½ cup freshly grated Parmesan cheese

8 oz. pancetta, prosciutto, or bacon, about 8 slices

olive oil, for cooking

1 garlic clove, crushed

freshly ground black pepper

to serve

extra freshly grated Parmesan cheese

freshly ground black pepper

serves 4–6

Crisp, garlic-scented bacon with a stream of creamy fresh eggs setting in the warm pasta, fragrant with the scent of freshly grated Parmesan. This is yet another of my favorite sauces, and one of the speciality dishes found in every simple eatery in Rome. The best, in my opinion, was at no-frills Carolina's restaurant, around the corner from my apartment in Piazza della Quercia. Carolina served the spaghetti carbonara of dreams, and this is her recipe.

Put the eggs and egg yolks in a bowl and mix lightly with a fork. Add the butter, cream, grated Parmesan, and lots of black pepper. Let stand without mixing.

Chop the pancetta into slivers. Cover the base of a medium skillet with olive oil and heat through. When it starts to haze, add the pancetta. When the fat starts to run, add the crushed garlic and stir well. Continue sautéing until the pancetta becomes crisp and golden.

Add the pancetta and pan juices to the freshly cooked pasta and mix vigorously. Beat the egg mixture lightly with a fork and pour over the pasta. Mix well and serve at once with extra cheese and plenty of freshly ground black pepper—the butter will melt and the eggs will cook in the heat of the pasta.

baby clam sauce
spaghettini alle vongole in bianco

Spaghettini with clams is typical of the regional cuisine of almost every coastal area, but I associate it most with Campania and vacations years ago on the Costa Amalfitana, in Positano, Ischia, and Capri. I remember balmy nights spent in waterside restaurants, diners oozing style, the sound of lapping water, and the chink of shells on the plate. This dish comes in two versions, *in bianco* (oil, garlic, and parsley) or *al pomodoro* (tomato sauce). There is also an easy pantry version I make at home, using jars of clams and canned tomatoes.

Wash the clams in plenty of running water until not a trace of sand is left. Drain well. Put them in a heavy saucepan over high heat. Cover with a lid and shake the pan until all the clams have opened. Strain off the liquid, pour it through a fine sieve, and reserve. Reduce if necessary.

Heat the olive oil in a large saucepan, add the garlic and pepper flakes, and heat through gently. When the garlic starts to turn golden, discard it and the pepper flakes. Add the clams to the pan, together with their strained cooking liquid. Add the parsley and cook gently for a minute or two for the flavors to blend.

Add the clams to the freshly cooked spaghettini and mix well. Tip onto a large serving plate and top with lots of black pepper, some more parsley, and olive oil. Serve at once.

Variation

Spaghettini con le vongole al pomodoro (with tomatoes)

Peel, seed, and chop 1 lb. plum tomatoes, then add to the oil at the same time as the garlic and chile. Cook over low heat for 20-30 minutes until reduced to a creamy mass. Add the clams and the strained juices and cook for a minute or so for the flavors to blend. Add the parsley and proceed as in the main recipe.

16 oz. spaghettini, freshly cooked

vongole sauce

2 lb. small fresh clams, in their shells

¹/₂–²/₃ cup olive oil

1 garlic clove, peeled but whole

½ teaspoon hot red pepper flakes

2 handfuls of parsley, finely chopped

to serve

freshly ground black pepper

freshly chopped parsley

extra virgin olive oil

serves 4–6

vegetables

There are an infinite number of pasta dishes that can be made with vegetables. Just take a basic sauce, such as melted butter; light cream, butter, and stock; olive oil and garlic or chile; tomato sauce; pesto—then add any lightly cooked vegetables. Vegetables can also be cooked from scratch with tomatoes, or sautéed in flavored oils, roasted, or cooked gently in melted butter and herbs.

pasta primavera
primavera

It doesn't matter where you are in Italy, somewhere, every morning barring Sunday you will find streets and squares crammed full of market stalls, spilling over with fresh vegetables picked that morning and proudly labeled *nostrani* (home produce). There is nothing like a vegetable grown in your own soil, then picked, cooked, and eaten on the same day. This is not impossible, even if you don't grow your own. Spend a little time seeking out a farmers' market near you. Vegetables need little cooking or adornment if they are young, sweet, and fresh. The harvest periods are short, so relish each vegetable in its season and reinvent this recipe—spring, summer, fall, and winter—as the crops change.

If using asparagus or green beans, cut them into 1-inch lengths. Cover the base of a skillet with olive oil and heat gently. Add the onion and sauté gently until softened and translucent. Add the wine and let bubble until evaporated. Stir in the green vegetables and tomatoes, then add salt and pepper to taste. Stir again, cover with a lid, and cook for 10–20 minutes or until tender. Stir in the herbs, then taste again for seasoning.

Add the sauce to the freshly cooked pasta, then add the grated Parmesan and strips of Parma ham, if using. Stir well and serve topped with basil leaves.

Variations

• Omit the Parma ham and use 2 oz. sun-dried tomatoes, thinly sliced, 1½ tablespoons capers, and 1½ tablespoons olives.

• Omit the Parma ham and add 1 tablespoon finely chopped anchovies, the finely chopped zest of 1 small unwaxed lemon, and a handful of parsley, finely chopped.

16 oz. pasta (any kind), freshly cooked

primavera sauce

olive oil, for cooking

1 onion, finely chopped

2 tablespoons white wine

1 lb. green vegetables, such as green beans, asparagus, peas, fava beans, or a mixture (shelled weight)

1 lb. ripe tomatoes, peeled, seeded, and chopped

a handful of mint, finely chopped

a handful of basil, finely chopped

3 tablespoons freshly grated Parmesan cheese, plus extra to serve

3–4 oz. Parma ham or prosciutto, cut into strips (optional)

sea salt and freshly ground black pepper

basil leaves, to serve

serves 4

roasted vegetables with capers and cherry tomatoes

verdura arrosta con capperi e pomodorini

16 oz. pasta, such as penne or rigatoni, freshly cooked

vegetable dressing

1 small eggplant, about 4 oz.

1 red bell pepper, halved and seeded

1 yellow bell pepper, halved and seeded

1 medium zucchini

2 small leeks, split and well washed

1½ tablespoons finely chopped rosemary leaves

2 garlic cloves, finely chopped

2 tablespoons olive oil

1–2 tablespoons capers, rinsed and drained

½ cup cherry tomatoes

to serve

extra virgin olive oil

6 sprigs of rosemary

freshly grated Parmesan cheese

a roasting pan

serves 4

When choosing bell peppers, eggplant, tomatoes, and the like, squeeze them lightly to ensure the flesh is firm. Don't worry if they're funny shapes, it's more important that they are fresh—even better if they have a bloom to them. When buying leeks, make sure you aren't paying a premium for a bunch of leaves and you have a good proportion of white trunk, the really tender, sweet part. Don't be put off by the leaves, however—as long as they are fresh, just cut them off and put them in the stockpot. Italians don't waste a thing and neither should any good cook.

Cut the eggplant, bell peppers, zucchini, and leeks into bite-size pieces, about 1 inch square, and arrange in a single layer in a roasting pan. Add the rosemary, garlic, and olive oil and mix well with your hands. Cover with foil, transfer to a preheated oven, and roast at 400°F for 20–30 minutes until tender.

Remove and discard the foil, add the capers and cherry tomatoes, stir well, and roast for a further 10 minutes.

Add the roasted vegetables to the freshly cooked pasta, stir well, and spread out on a serving plate. Sprinkle with oil and rosemary and serve with Parmesan.

Variations

• Instead of cherry tomatoes, add 3 tablespoons black olives.

• Experiment with other kinds of vegetables.

zucchini and toasted pine nuts with olive oil and parsley

zucchine, olio d'oliva, pinoli tostati e prezzemolo

This recipe comes originally from Sicily, where the colorful regional cooking abounds with vegetable-based recipes enhanced by the island's glorious olive oil. The quality of the oil in this dish is as important as the freshness of the zucchini. I use an extra virgin olive oil for all my cooking, other than deep-frying, but I also keep a bottle of something special for dishes like this.

Spread out the pine nuts on a baking tray and cook under a medium-hot broiler or in a preheated oven at 400°F until golden—this will only take a few minutes, so watch carefully, because they can burn quickly. Turn them once. When brown, remove from the heat, spread out on a plate, and let cool. Alternatively, toast them in a dry skillet as described on page 18.

Heat the olive oil and garlic in a large skillet and, when the garlic starts to turn golden, discard it. Add the zucchini and stir-fry quickly until golden. Add salt and pepper to taste.

Add the zucchini and their cooking oil to the freshly cooked pasta. Stir well, sprinkle with chopped parsley and the toasted pine nuts, and serve.

16 oz. spaghettini, freshly cooked

vegetable dressing
½ cup good olive oil
1 garlic clove, peeled and whole
5–6 baby zucchini, thinly sliced
sea salt and freshly ground black pepper

to serve
a handful of parsley, finely chopped
a handful of pine nuts, about 1 oz.

a baking sheet with sides

serves 4

8 oz. pasta, such as tubetti, spirali, or penne, freshly cooked

black bean sauce

⅔ cup small dried black beans or 15 oz. canned black beans

olive oil, for cooking

1 carrot, finely chopped

1 small onion, finely chopped

½ celery stalk, finely chopped

2 garlic cloves, crushed

15 oz. canned plum tomatoes, drained (reserve juice), seeded, and chopped

½ teaspoon hot red pepper flakes or ⅓ cinnamon stick

sea salt and freshly ground black pepper

garlic-fried breadcrumbs

3 tablespoons olive oil

½ cup fresh bread crumbs

1 teaspoon finely chopped fresh rosemary leaves

1 garlic clove, finely chopped

to serve

a large handful of arugula

1 cup Parmesan cheese shavings

serves 4–6 as an appetizer

chile and black bean sauce with garlic-fried bread crumbs

I love beans of every sort, but not so my family. Consequently, all those delicious Italian winter warmers like *pasta e fagioli* remain pretty much locked away in the pages of my Italian cookbooks. Last summer, I encountered small black beans for the first time in the local natural food store: it was love at first sight. They are the culinary equivalent of the little black dress. I had to have them—but how to serve the beans to the unconverted? Tomato sauce and garlic-fried bread crumbs are favorites in our house, so I had finally served up beans that weren't picked out and left on the plate!

If using dried beans, soak them overnight in plenty of cold water. Next day, drain them, rinse well, put in a saucepan, cover with cold water, and bring to a boil. Do not add salt. Boil hard for 15 minutes, then drain and rinse. If using canned beans instead, drain and rinse them, too.

Cover the base of a medium saucepan with olive oil, then heat gently. Add the carrot, onion, celery, garlic, and beans and stir gently in the oil for 5 minutes, or until the vegetables soften. Add the tomatoes and pepper flakes or cinnamon and stir again. Heat to simmering point, cover with a lid, and cook over very low heat for 30 minutes, stirring from time to time. It may be necessary to add a little reserved tomato juice to keep the sauce moist. Add salt and pepper to taste and discard the cinnamon stick, if using.

To make the garlic-fried bread crumbs, heat the 3 tablespoons olive oil in a skillet. Put the bread crumbs, garlic, and rosemary in a bowl and mix well. When the oil starts to haze, add the bread crumb mixture and sauté until crisp and golden. Transfer to a plate lined with paper towels, let drain, and cool.

Add the sauce and arugula to the freshly cooked pasta, stir well, and serve topped with garlic-fried bread crumbs and Parmesan shavings.

cauliflower and broccoli arabesque
con i broccoli

This unusual vegetable sauce, enhanced with golden raisins, anchovies, and pine nuts, explodes with flavors. It is based on a classic recipe popular in parts of southern Italy and Sicily, where ingredients such as raisins and pine nuts show an Arab influence— *arabesque*. It can also be served as a side dish with meat and fish. There is a huge selection of vegetables to choose from, so try one or more types and vary them according to season.

Put the pine nuts in a dry skillet and heat gently until golden brown all over. Take care, because they burn easily. Remove to a plate and let cool.

Soak the golden raisins in boiling water for 15 minutes, then drain and pat dry with paper towels. Cook the cauliflower, broccoli, broccoli rabe, and/or cime di rape in a large saucepan of boiling salted water until just soft, 5-10 minutes. Drain well.

Put the tomato paste in a small bowl, add the warm water, and stir to dilute. Heat half the olive oil in a sauté pan, then add the onion and tomato mixture. Cook over low heat until softened, then add the boiled vegetables.

Mash the anchovies in a small bowl, then stir in the hot milk and remaining olive oil to form a smooth paste. Pour over the vegetables, add the golden raisins and pine nuts, stir well, and cover with a lid. Turn off the heat and set aside to develop the flavors.

Add the sauce to the pasta, stir well, then transfer to a large serving dish. Add the cilantro and extra pine nuts. Serve at once with grated pecorino.

Variation

Omit the anchovies and add 3 tablespoons black olive paste or 3 tablespoons capers, rinsed and drained.

16 oz. pasta, such as spaghettini or orecchiette, freshly cooked

calabrese sauce

$^2/_3$ cup pine nuts (2$^1/_2$ oz. package), plus extra to serve

$^1/_3$ cup golden raisins

1$^1/_2$ lb. cruciferous vegetables, such as cauliflower or broccoli, separated into florets, broccoli rabe, cime di rape, or a mixture of several

1$^1/_2$ tablespoons tomato paste

$^1/_2$ cup warm water

$^1/_2$ cup olive oil

1 onion, finely sliced

1 small can anchovies, (2 oz.), drained thoroughly and patted dry with paper towels

$^1/_4$ cup scalding hot milk

to serve

torn cilantro leaves or parsley

freshly grated pecorino or Parmesan cheese

serves 4

mushroom cream sauce
with garlic, parsley, and marsala
al geo

8 oz. pasta, such as pappardelle, tagliatelle, fettucine, or farfalle, freshly cooked

mushroom sauce

4 tablespoons unsalted butter

1 garlic clove, crushed

a handful of parsley, chopped

2 cups thinly sliced button mushrooms

3 tablespoons Marsala wine or sherry

½ cup vegetable or chicken stock

1 cup light cream

3 tablespoons freshly grated Parmesan cheese

sea salt and freshly ground black pepper

to serve

freshly chopped parsley

freshly grated Parmesan cheese

serves 4

This is a rich, aromatic cream sauce flavored with mushrooms, ever-so-slowly cooked with garlic, parsley, and Marsala. I learned to make it in Bologna from Tina Monetti, who was my "Italian Mamma" and culinary inspiration when I first lived in Italy as a teenage student. It has remained a firm favorite. The sauce also goes well with pan-fried steak, veal, and pork. Keep a bottle of Marsala in the pantry for cooking—it has a very distinctive flavor and is useful for both sweet and savory dishes. It is used frequently in Bolognese cooking, and in Sicily where it is made.

To make the mushroom sauce, melt the butter in a skillet. Add the garlic, parsley, and mushrooms and cook gently over low heat, stirring from time to time.

When the mushrooms have reduced and starting to soften, add the Marsala and salt and pepper to taste. Stir well, cover the skillet with a lid, and let cook for a further 30 minutes, adding a little stock from time to time. The mushrooms should be moist, but not watery. Add the cream and heat gently, shaking the skillet from time to time.

Add the sauce and the Parmesan to the freshly cooked pasta. Sprinkle with chopped parsley and serve at once with extra Parmesan.

Variation

Cook small cubes of eggplant instead of mushrooms.

fish and shellfish

Shellfish works well *in bianco* (with olive oil, chile, and parsley) or *al pomodoro* (with tomato). Do take care when combining fish with tomato sauce, because too much tomato will completely mask the taste of the fish. Smoked fish such as salmon goes well with cream, as do scallops and fresh salmon. Milder fish suit melted butter or olive oil and crisp vegetables.

16 oz. spaghettini, freshly cooked

seafood sauce

10 oz. small squid

10 oz. small clams, in the shell

10 oz. mussels, in the shell

10 oz. shrimp

other fish or seafood, to taste

olive oil, for cooking

a handful of fresh parsley, chopped

a piece of dried chile, to taste

4 garlic cloves, finely chopped

⅔ cup white wine

sea salt and freshly ground black pepper

to serve

a handful of parsley, finely chopped

extra virgin olive oil

serves 4–6

fishmarket sauce
frutti di mare

This is the mother of all seafood sauces, a favorite in practically every beach and harbor restaurant in Italy. The success of seafood sauce depends very much on the freshness and variety of fish, which is why I love making it on vacation. The joy of cooking while at the shore in Italy is that, however tiny the kitchen, there is always a splendid collection of pots and pans that really make you want to cook Italian. Stir the sauce into pasta or risotto or serve it with bread.

Clean the fish and seafood as necessary. Scrub the clams and mussels, rinse thoroughly in cold running water, and drain well. Discard any that remain open. Cut the squid into rings (very small squid can be cooked whole).

Cover the base of a large skillet or large saucepan with olive oil, then set over medium heat. Add the chopped parsley, chile, and garlic and cook until soft. Increase the heat, add the white wine, and let bubble until evaporated.

Add the squid and sauté for a few minutes, then add the clams and mussels, cover, and shake the pan until all the shells have opened (discard any that will not open). Add the shrimp and cook for a few more minutes until they become opaque—no longer, or they will be tough and tasteless. Add salt and pepper to taste. Remove the pan from the heat and set aside, covered with the lid, to develop the flavors.

Add half the sauce to the freshly cooked pasta and mix well. Spoon the remaining sauce on top, add the chopped parsley and olive oil, and serve at once.

monkfish and italian vegetables with olives and capers

coda di rospo e verdure con olive e capperi

16 oz. pasta, such as farfalle or tagliatelle, freshly cooked

monkfish and vegetables

1 lb. monkfish tail

¼ cup good olive oil

2 shallots, finely chopped

3–4 baby zucchini, cut into bite-size pieces

1 large red bell pepper, about 8 oz., halved, seeded, and cut into bite-size pieces

½ cup white wine

2½ tablespoons capers

2 small tomatoes, about 8 oz., peeled, seeded, and chopped

1½ tablespoons pitted black olives

sea salt and freshly ground black pepper

to serve

25 basil leaves or a handful of parsley, finely chopped

extra virgin olive oil

a shallow roasting pan, oiled

serves 4–6

One of the highlights of a vacation in Italy is an early morning visit to a fish market. It's fascinating to watch the fishermen, restaurateurs, porters, agents in suits trading by cellphone, and the odd savvy housewife, all padding around the wet floors sizing up the morning's catch. Whole tuna and swordfish, boxes of squid and shrimp of every size and variety, ray and turbot, scabbard fish coiled into boxes like ties in a drawer, small sharks with eerie gray skin, and the extraordinary monkfish, cowled in more fleshy folds than a bloodhound. This is fresh!

Wipe the fish and cut into 4 equal pieces, discarding any bones. Season well with salt and pepper, arrange in an oiled roasting pan, and set aside.

Heat the oil in a skillet, then add the shallots. Cook until soft, then raise the heat, add the zucchini and bell pepper, and brown quickly. Add the wine, and when it has evaporated, add the capers, stir well, and add salt and pepper to taste.

Spoon the cooked vegetables over the fish in the roasting pan until covered, then add the chopped tomatoes, olives, and extra olive oil. Cover the pan with foil and cook in a preheated oven at 400°F for 8 minutes. Remove from the oven, discard the foil, cut the fish into bite-size pieces, and mix carefully into the vegetables.

Add the fish and vegetables and their cooking juices to the pasta and mix well, then stir in the basil or parsley and oil.

Variations

• Try thick cod, halibut, salmon, or haddock fillets rather than monkfish tails.

• Use leeks, fennel bulbs, mushrooms, and eggplant instead of bell peppers and zucchini.

tuna, coriander, and lemon zest with tomato salad

*tonno, coriandolo e limone
con pomodoro concasse*

This is a delicious lunch or supper dish with ingredients that, though not all strictly from the pantry, are to be found in most kitchens.

To prepare the salad, cut a cross in the top and bottom of the tomatoes, then plunge them briefly into boiling water. Drain, pull off the skins, then remove the seeds and cores. Cut the flesh into small cubes. Add the oil, mint, salt, and pepper to taste and set aside to develop the flavors.

To make the sauce, cover the base of a skillet with olive oil, add the onions and coriander seeds, and cook slowly over medium heat. When the onions start to soften, add 3 tablespoons water and cover with a lid. Continue cooking over low heat until soft. This will take 15 minutes—do not rush (add extra water if necessary).

When the onions are very soft, add the tuna, capers, if using, lemon zest, lots of black pepper, and half the milk. Stir well, cover again, and cook for 10 minutes over low heat (add the remaining milk if necessary).

Add the sauce and the tomato salad to the freshly cooked pasta and mix well. Sprinkle with mint sprigs and serve at once.

Variation

Use 1 pint cherry tomatoes, cut in half, instead of the tomato salad.

16 oz. pasta, such as tagliatelle, conchiglie, or farfalle, freshly cooked

tomato salad

4 firm tomatoes

3 tablespoons olive oil

1½ tablespoons freshly chopped mint or parsley

sea salt and freshly ground black pepper

sauce

olive oil, for cooking

2 onions, finely sliced

1 teaspoon crushed coriander seeds

2 cans of tuna in oil, 6 oz. each, lightly drained

1½ tablespoons capers (optional)

grated zest of 1 unwaxed lemon

½ cup milk

sea salt and freshly ground black pepper

a handful of mint sprigs, to serve

serves 4–6

grilled shrimp and salmon with basil and citrus cream sauce

*salmone e gamberi ai ferri
con panna, basilico e limone*

8 oz. egg pasta, such as pappardelle or tagliatelle, freshly cooked

shrimp and salmon sauce

4 oz. cooked peeled Northern pink shrimp, plus 6 oz. shell-on (uncooked) Northern pink shrimp

1 cup light cream

3 tablespoons unsalted butter

8 oz. thick salmon fillet, cut into thin slices across the grain of the fish

finely chopped zest of 1 lemon and freshly squeezed juice of ½

olive oil, to taste

a large handful of basil leaves, finely sliced

sea salt and freshly ground black pepper

a preheated stove-top grill pan

serves 4

I came across the combination of cream, fish, and basil on Giglio, a tiny island off the coast of Tuscany. After more than twenty hairpin bends high above sea level, there is a medieval fortress from where, on a clear day, you can see Corsica, Elba, Monte Cristo, and mainland Italy. Outside of the fortress walls, there is abundant spring water and a patchwork of tiny fertile garden plots where basil leaves grow the size of spinach. Inside the walls is a tangle of tiny streets and stairways hiding a variety of restaurants that burst into life after dark. Here, away from the suffocating heat and the hustle and bustle of the port below, visitors and islanders enjoy splendid food, including delicious local fish and homemade pasta.

Put the 4 oz. peeled shrimp in a food processor and blend to a paste. Put the cream, butter, and freshly ground black pepper in a small saucepan and heat gently, shaking the pan from time to time. When the sauce has thickened, add the shrimp paste to the cream, stir, cover, and switch off the heat.

Preheat a stove-top grill pan until very hot. Arrange the strips of salmon across the ridges of the pan and cook quickly on both sides. Transfer the pieces to a plate as they brown, sprinkle with oil, lemon juice, salt, and pepper.

Pan-grill the shell-on shrimp, in batches if necessary, until aromatic and opaque. Do not overcook or they will be tough and tasteless. Set aside 8–12 shrimp and 4 slices of the salmon for serving.

Add the sauce, shrimp, salmon pieces, and basil to the freshly cooked pasta and mix well. Divide between 4 pasta bowls. Make small piles of the reserved shrimp and salmon on the top of each portion and sprinkle with lemon zest. Serve at once.

meat and poultry

The joy of meat sauces is that they are popular with almost everyone. They improve when made in advance, so they can simply be reheated in the time it takes to cook the pasta. They keep well and freeze well, so always make a double quantity, serve half with this pasta and use the remainder with lasagne or risotto.

bacon, chile, and tomatoes
amatriciana

This recipe comes originally from Le Marche (pronounced "lay MAR-kay") region of Italy, but it is also synonymous with the robust traditional cooking of Rome. For me, it is reminiscent of the many evenings whiled away enjoying wholesome food in simple surroundings. The sauce is made with fried pancetta and onions, flavored with chile, and cooked in tomato. Traditionally, it is served with bucatini, thick spaghetti-like pasta with a hole running though the middle.

Cover the base of a skillet with olive oil, then set over medium heat until a haze starts to rise. Add the pancetta and the pepper flakes. Cook until the pancetta fat runs, then add the onion. Sauté over low heat until transparent.

Add the tomatoes, cover, and cook over low heat for 30 minutes. Stir often to prevent sticking, adding a little of the tomato juice to the pan if necessary. Add salt and pepper to taste. At this stage the sauce can be rested and reheated when required.

When ready to serve, cook the pasta, then stir in the sauce, the 3 tablespoons cheese, and parsley. Sprinkle with extra oil and serve at once with extra cheese.

16 oz. pasta, such as bucatini, spaghetti, or penne, freshly cooked

bacon, chile, and tomato sauce

olive oil, for cooking

8 oz. prosciutto or bacon, cut into thin strips

1/2 teaspoon hot red pepper flakes, to taste

1 onion, finely chopped

2 cans whole peeled tomatoes, about 14 oz. each, drained (retain the juice), seeded, and chopped

3 tablespoons freshly grated pecorino or Parmesan cheese

sea salt and freshly ground black pepper

to serve

a handful of parsley, chopped

extra virgin olive oil

extra freshly grated Parmesan

serves 4–6

herbed chicken with garlic bread crumbs
pollo con maggiorana

16 oz. pasta, such as wide pappardelle, farfalle, or rigatoni, freshly cooked

freshly grated Parmesan cheese, to serve (optional)

herbed chicken sauce

10 oz. chicken thighs, boneless and skinless

2 oz. pancetta, prosciutto, or bacon (about 2 slices)

a handful of parsley

3 tablespoons olive oil

¼ cup white wine

1 small garlic clove, finely chopped

2 teaspoons chopped fresh marjoram leaves or a pinch of dried marjoram

1 can whole tomatoes, about 14 oz., drained, seeded, and chopped

sea salt and freshly ground black pepper

garlic bread crumbs

¼ cup olive oil

½ cup fresh bread crumbs

1 teaspoon finely chopped fresh marjoram

1 garlic clove, finely chopped

serves 4–6

Garlic bread crumbs are served with pasta all over the *meridione* (southern Italy) instead of cheese, particularly with old-fashioned traditional dishes such as *vermicelli alla carrettiere*. This goes back to the days when every region had to rely totally on its own produce. The south was very poor indeed and there was no dairy farming to speak of, so consequently little or no cheese, but every household would have some stale bread. Durum wheat provided the flour. A few goats and sheep provided what little meat there was in "richer" areas. There was of course olive oil, but not the liquid gold we are used to—more a cloudy, somewhat rancid concoction, crudely forced from the olives. Having survived these conditions, it is not surprising that the Italian cook wastes nothing. Necessity, in Italy, was indeed the mamma of invention and of their rich culinary heritage.

To make the herbed chicken, cut each chicken thigh into 6-10 bite-size pieces. Put the pancetta and parsley together and chop finely. Heat the oil in a heavy saucepan, add the chopped mixture, and sauté over low heat until transparent. Add the chicken pieces and sauté until brown. Add the white wine and heat until evaporated. Add the garlic, marjoram, tomatoes, and salt and pepper to taste. Cover with a lid and cook gently for 30 minutes. Stir from time to time. At this stage the sauce can be rested and reheated when required.

To make the garlic bread crumbs, heat the olive oil in a second skillet. Put the bread crumbs, marjoram, and garlic in a bowl and mix well. When the oil starts to haze, add the bread crumb mixture and sauté until crisp and golden. Transfer to a plate covered with paper towels and let drain and cool. Add the sauce to the pasta and mix well. Sprinkle with garlic bread crumbs, and serve with cheese, if using.

meatballs in tomato sauce
polpettine al sugo di pomodoro

I can't think of meatballs in tomato sauce with pasta without thinking of that crazy old song "On top of Old Smoky, all covered with cheese, I first lost my meatball when somebody sneezed. It rolled off the table …" Meatballs in tomato sauce are synonymous with early immigrants to the US from southern Italy—and no wonder, because it still plays an important part in the food of this region.

To make the tomato sauce, cover the base of a skillet with olive oil and heat gently. Add the onion, carrot, and celery and cook over low heat until soft. Do not let brown. Add the tomatoes and basil, season with salt and pepper, cover with a lid, and cook for 30 minutes. Stir from time to time, adding a little reserved tomato juice if necessary.

To make the meatballs, put the meat, cheese, bread, parsley, garlic, egg, red wine, salt, and pepper in a bowl. Mix well and refrigerate for 1 hour. Take small teaspoons of the mixture and roll into tiny balls, flouring your hands as you work.

The meatballs may be deep-fried or sautéed in batches in vegetable oil. If using a deep-fryer, follow the manufacturer's instructions.

As each meatball is done, remove with a slotted spoon and drain on paper towels. When all the meatballs have been cooked and drained, put them in the tomato sauce and cook over gentle heat for 10 minutes. At this point, the sauce can be set aside and reheated when required.

When ready to serve, add the reheated sauce and the ½ cup pecorino to the freshly cooked pasta and mix well. Top with basil and serve with extra cheese.

Variation

Use the same quantity of beef or veal, or 3 oz. turkey and 1 oz. ham, instead of the pork.

16 oz. pasta, such as rigatone or bucatini, freshly cooked

tomato sauce

olive oil, for cooking

1 small onion, finely chopped

1 small carrot, finely chopped

½ celery stalk, finely chopped

2 cans Italian plum tomatoes, about 14 oz. each, drained (retain the juices), seeded, and chopped

20 fresh basil leaves

½ cup freshly grated pecorino cheese

sea salt and freshly ground black pepper

meatballs

4 oz. lean ground pork, ¼ cup

50 g freshly grated pecorino cheese

1–2 crusty Italian dinner rolls, soaked in milk and squeezed dry

a handful of parsley, chopped

1 garlic clove, finely chopped

1 egg

1 tablespoon red wine

sea salt and freshly ground black pepper

all-purpose flour, for rolling

vegetable oil, for cooking

to serve

extra pecorino cheese

basil leaves

serves 4–6

light ligurian meat sauce with tomato, mushrooms, and pine nuts

la bagna de carne

16 oz. pasta, such as homemade trenette or ravioli, or tagliatelle, ridged penne, or spaghettini, freshly cooked

light meat sauce

½ oz. dried porcini mushrooms

milk (see method)

3 tablespoons olive oil

1 onion, finely chopped

4 oz. lean ground beef

⅓ cup pine nuts

1 can peeled tomatoes, about 14 oz., drained (reserve the juices), seeded, and chopped

1 tablespoon finely chopped mixed rosemary and thyme

3 tablespoons freshly grated Parmesan cheese

sea salt and freshly ground black pepper

to serve

1 teaspoon freshly chopped rosemary

1 teaspoon freshly chopped thyme

extra freshly grated Parmesan cheese

serves 4–6

This meat sauce is from Liguria and differs from the rich *ragù* from Bologna (page 17). It is a light *sugo*, typical of the cooking of this region. A small amount of meat is swelled with tomatoes, mushrooms, and pine nuts, enough to dress one pound of pasta. Traditionally, it would be served with homemade trenette or ravioli.

Put the mushrooms in a bowl, add enough milk to cover, then soak for 15 minutes. Squeeze them dry and chop finely. Discard the milk.

Heat the olive oil in a large saucepan, add the onion, and cook over low heat until soft. Increase the heat, add the meat, and sauté until browned. Add the pine nuts, mushrooms, tomatoes, herbs, salt, and pepper, stir well, and cover with a lid. Reduce the heat and cook slowly for 1 hour. Stir at regular intervals and, if necessary, add a little of the reserved tomato juice to keep the sauce moist.

Add the sauce and Parmesan to the freshly cooked pasta and mix well. Serve at once sprinkled with extra herbs. Serve extra cheese separately.

country sausage, peas, and tomatoes
piselli, salsiccia e pomodorini

This version of a traditional country recipe uses Italian sausages rather than pancetta or prosciutto as its base. The contrast in flavor and texture of the meaty coarse sausage, the sweetness of the peas, and colorful cherry tomatoes works very well. Make sure you use a coarse-textured Italian-type sausage.

Cover the base of a skillet with olive oil, then set over medium heat. Add the sausages and cook over low heat, turning until they are brown on all sides. Pour off the excess fat and reserve. Cut the sausages in half, scrape out the meat, and discard the skins. Add a little stock and deglaze the pan. Stir the resulting pan juices into the sausage meat. Simmer for a few minutes. The whole process will take about 20–30 minutes.

Pour a little of the reserved sausage fat into a clean skillet and heat through. Add the onion and cook over gentle heat until soft. Add the peas, confectioners' sugar, parsley, and enough stock to cover the ingredients. Cover with a lid and cook until the peas are tender. If using frozen peas, add them to the onions with ⅛ cup stock and heat through.

Stir the peas into the sausage meat and let simmer for 5 minutes. When ready to serve, increase the heat, add the tomatoes, and cook quickly until the edges start to wilt. Add the sauce to the freshly cooked pasta, stir in the Parmesan, and mix well. Serve with extra cheese.

Variation

Instead of the peas, stir in cooked white or other beans after cooking the onion. Add a few chopped tomatoes and cook for 10–15 minutes or until the tomatoes are thick and creamy. Proceed as in the main recipe.

16 oz. pasta, such as ridged penne, or tubetti, freshly cooked

sauce

olive oil, for cooking

8 sweet Italian-type sausages

1 cup stock, such as chicken, beef, or vegetable

1 small onion, finely chopped

2 cups. fresh shelled peas, or 1½ cups frozen peas

1 teaspoon confectioners' sugar

a handful of parsley, chopped

1 pint cherry tomatoes, halved

3 tablespoons freshly grated Parmesan cheese, plus extra, to serve

serves 4–6

cream, cheese, and eggs

Cream sauces are delicious on their own, enriched with cheese, herbs, or citrus zest and stirred into egg-based or stuffed pastas. They are useful as a base—simply add smoked fish or meat, cooked poultry or game, lightly boiled vegetables or nuts, to create a feast out of very little. Cheese sauces are versatile, because they can be prepared in less time than it takes to cook the pasta. Just about any cheese goes well with pasta, whether grated, shaved, or melted.

basic cream sauce with butter and parmesan

panna, burro e parmigiano

This basic sauce provides the departure point for a variety of other sauces. Stir in some poultry, fish, or vegetables as a feast for unexpected guests. Add herbs, nuts, or cheese to make a delicious sauce for stuffed pasta. Always dress the pasta in a bowl rather than the pan, because the heat of the pan will dry out dairy-based sauces.

Put the cream and butter in a shallow saucepan over low heat. Bring to simmering point, shaking the pan from time to time. Let simmer for a few minutes or until the sauce starts to thicken. Add the cheese and pepper or nutmeg and stir.

Stir the sauce and half of the water or stock into the pasta. Mix until well coated. Add extra water or stock if necessary and stir again. Serve at once with extra Parmesan, chopped herbs, and grated lemon zest, if using.

Variation

Add 4 oz. finely sliced smoked salmon or trout and 3 tablespoons finely chopped dill or fennel to the pasta at the same time as the cream sauce, and stir gently.

8 oz. egg-based pasta
or 1 package of stuffed pasta,
freshly cooked

basic cream sauce

1 cup light cream

2 tablespoons unsalted butter

3 tablespoons freshly grated
Parmesan cheese

lots of black pepper or freshly
grated nutmeg

2–4 tablespoons pasta cooking
water or stock

to serve (optional)

freshly grated Parmesan cheese

3 tablespoons finely chopped
herbs, such as parsley, fennel,
cilantro, or basil

freshly grated zest of
1/2 unwaxed lemon

serves 4

béchamel sauce with prosciutto, emmental, and salad leaves
la besciamella con lattuga, prosciutto cotto e emmental

16 oz. farfalle or ridged penne, freshly cooked

béchamel sauce

2 tablespoons unsalted butter

2 tablespoons all-purpose flour

1 cup warm milk

salt

freshly grated nutmeg

vegetables

2 tablespoons unsalted butter

1 small onion, finely chopped

½ head iceberg lettuce, shredded

½ nutmeg, freshly grated

4 oz. cooked ham, sliced into thin strips

sea salt and freshly ground black pepper

to serve

1 cup Emmental cheese shavings

freshly grated Parmesan cheese

serves 4–6

Cold ham and salad never tasted as good as this simple supper dish. Finely shredded Savoy cabbage, leeks, or bok choy can be used instead of iceberg lettuce. Vegetarians might like to add 1 cup chopped walnuts instead of ham. Béchamel is a very versatile base sauce to which all kinds of ingredients can be added.

To make the béchamel sauce, put the butter in a saucepan and melt until it starts to bubble. Add the flour and mix well. Cook over gentle heat for 1-2 minutes, add the milk, and continue cooking until the sauce thickens. Stir constantly with a wire whisk to stop lumps forming. Add salt and grated nutmeg to taste.

To cook the vegetables, gently melt the butter in a large skillet. Add the onion and sauté over low heat until transparent. Add the lettuce and continue cooking for 5 minutes. Grate the nutmeg onto the lettuce and onion as it is cooking. When the lettuce is well wilted, add the ham and béchamel sauce and stir. Add salt and pepper to taste.

Add the sauce to the pasta and mix until well coated. Sprinkle with Emmental shavings and serve grated Parmesan separately.

Variation

Instead of lettuce, use 1 lb. (2-3 cups) sliced mushrooms sautéed in butter with thyme and garlic, add to the béchamel, and serve with Parmesan shavings.

cherry tomatoes and mozzarella with arugula, garlic, and olive oil
pasta estiva

This colorful summer dish is perfect for alfresco eating. It is more a salad than a sauce—just stir it into hot pasta and serve warm.

Put the mozzarella and cherry tomatoes in a large bowl. Add the olive oil, plenty of salt, and freshly ground black pepper to taste, then mix.

Add the hot pasta to the mozzarella salad and mix well. Add the arugula, turn once, then spoon onto a flat serving dish. Sprinkle with olive oil and balsamic vinegar and serve warm.

Variation

Add toasted pine nuts or finely chopped garlic to the mozzarella and tomatoes. Finely chop 2 handfuls parsley, mint, and basil, and use instead of the arugula. Omit the balsamic vinegar.

16 oz. pasta, such as farfalle or small tubetti, freshly cooked

tomato mozzarella dressing

8 oz. baby fresh mozzarella cheeses, drained and halved

2 cups cherry tomatoes, halved

1/4 cup good olive oil

a large handful of arugula

sea salt and freshly ground black pepper

to serve

extra virgin olive oil

balsamic vinegar

serves 4–6

ricotta, cinnamon, and walnuts
ricotta e noci

16 oz. pasta, such as spaghettini, linguine, or ridged penne, freshly cooked

ricotta dressing

1 cup ricotta cheese

3 tablespoons unsalted butter, softened

1 teaspoon confectioners' sugar

1 teaspoon ground cinnamon or apple pie spice

½ cup pasta cooking water

½ cup chopped walnuts

sea salt and freshly ground black pepper

to serve

1½ tablespoons chopped walnuts

freshly grated Parmesan cheese

serves 4–6

A delicate and original appetizer for a party and an ideal vegetarian meal—this is more a dressing than a sauce, because there is no cooking. So simple, it can be prepared in the time it takes to cook the pasta. The combination of sweet and savory elements dates back to Roman times and remained popular until the seventeenth century. Honey, butter, cheese, and sweet spices were put together in all sorts of dishes and may well have constituted the first pasta dressing, each ingredient being added separately.

Put the ricotta, butter, confectioners' sugar, and cinnamon in a bowl and beat with a wooden spoon until smooth and creamy. Add salt and pepper to taste and stir in half the pasta water.

Add the ricotta mixture to the pasta, add the remaining pasta water if necessary, then stir in the chopped walnuts. Mix well until coated. Serve at once with the extra walnuts and Parmesan.

Variation

Try toasted pine nuts or almonds instead of walnuts.

index

conversion charts

Weights and measures have been rounded up or down slightly to make measuring easier.

Volume equivalents:

American	Metric	Imperial
1 teaspoon	5 ml	
1 tablespoon	15 ml	
¼ cup	60 ml	2 fl.oz.
⅓ cup	75 ml	2½ fl.oz.
½ cup	125 ml	4 fl.oz.
⅔ cup	150 ml	5 fl.oz. (¼ pint)
¾ cup	175 ml	6 fl.oz.
1 cup	250 ml	8 fl.oz.

Weight equivalents:

Imperial	Metric
1 oz.	25 g
2 oz.	50 g
3 oz.	75 g
4 oz.	125 g
5 oz.	150 g
6 oz.	175 g
7 oz.	200 g
8 oz. (½ lb.)	250 g
9 oz.	275 g
10 oz.	300 g
11 oz.	325 g
12 oz.	375 g
13 oz.	400 g
14 oz.	425 g
15 oz.	475 g
16 oz. (1 lb.)	500 g
2 lb.	1 kg

Measurements:

Inches	Cm
¼ inch	5 mm
½ inch	1 cm
¾ inch	1.5 cm
1 inch	2.5 cm
2 inches	5 cm
3 inches	7 cm
4 inches	10 cm
5 inches	12 cm
6 inches	15 cm
7 inches	18 cm
8 inches	20 cm
9 inches	23 cm
10 inches	25 cm
11 inches	28 cm
12 inches	30 cm

Oven temperatures:

110°C	(225°F)	Gas ¼
120°C	(250°F)	Gas ½
140°C	(275°F)	Gas 1
150°C	(300°F)	Gas 2
160°C	(325°F)	Gas 3
180°C	(350°F)	Gas 4
190°C	(375°F)	Gas 5
200°C	(400°F)	Gas 6
220°C	(425°F)	Gas 7
230°C	(450°F)	Gas 8
240°C	(475°F)	Gas 9